Watch It Grow

An Apple's Life

Nancy Dickmann

Heinemann Library
Chicago, Illinois

www.capstonepub.com
Visit our website to find out more information about Heinemann-Raintree books.

To order:
☎ Phone 800-747-4992
🖳 Visit www.capstonepub.com to browse our catalog and order online.

Edited by Rebecca Rissman, Nancy Dickmann, and Catherine Veitch
Designed by Joanna Hinton-Malivoire
Picture research by Mica Brancic
Production by Victoria Fitzgerald
Originated by Capstone Global Library Ltd

Library of Congress Cataloging-in-Publication Data
Dickmann, Nancy.
 An apple's life / Nancy Dickmann. -- 1st ed.
   p. cm. -- (Watch it grow)
 Includes bibliographical references and index.
 ISBN 978-1-4329-4141-3 (hc) -- ISBN 978-1-4329-4150-5 (pb) 1. Apples-
-Juvenile literature. I. Title. II. Series: Dickmann, Nancy. Watch it grow.
 SB363.D54 2010
 634'.11--dc22
                                2009049157

Acknowledgments
We would would like to thank the following for permission to reproduce photographs: Alamy: imageBROKER, 13, Mode Images Limited, 9, 23 middle, Nigel Cattlin, 10, 22 right, 23 bottom; FLPA: Nigel Cattlin, 8; iStockphoto: brainmaster, 17, 22 bottom, dmitry_7, back cover, 15, ericmichaud, 4, gaffera, 5, 22 left, intst, 12, lillisphotography, 7, ManicBlu, cover inset, 20, 22 top, patty_c, 19, Viorika, cover; Shutterstock: Constant, 11, dimid_86, 18, Fotokostic, 21, gorillaimages, 16, 23 top, Toms Z, 14, Valeri Potapova, 6

The publisher would like to thank Nancy Harris for her assistance in the preparation of this book.

Every effort has been made to contact copyright holders of material reproduced in this book. Any omissions will be rectified in subsequent printings if notice is given to the publisher.

Contents

Life Cycles

All living things have a life cycle.

An apple has a life cycle.

seed

Inside an apple there are seeds.
The seeds will grow into a new
apple tree.

The new apple tree will grow apples.
The life cycle starts again.

Seeds and Shoots

An apple seed grows in the ground.

roots

Roots grow down from the seed into the ground.

shoot

A shoot grows up from the seed.

leaves

Leaves grow from the shoot.

Becoming a Tree

The young tree needs water and sunlight to grow.

The young tree grows bigger.

The tree grows new leaves in
the spring.

flower

The tree grows flowers in the spring.

Making Apples

pollen

A bee comes to feed on a flower.
The bee has pollen on it.

The pollen helps make new apple
seeds grow on the tree.

Then an apple starts to grow.

When the apples have grown, some
fall from the tree.

seed

The apple has seeds inside it.

The life cycle starts again.

Life Cycle of an Apple Tree

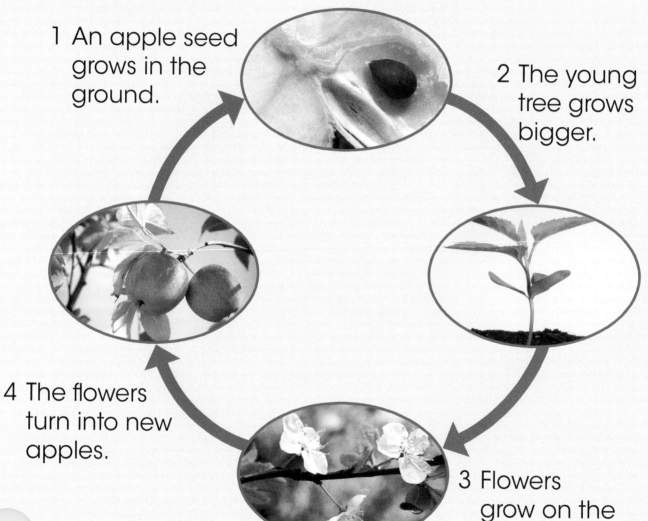

1 An apple seed grows in the ground.

2 The young tree grows bigger.

3 Flowers grow on the apple tree.

4 The flowers turn into new apples.

Picture Glossary

 **pollen** yellow powder inside a flower

 **root** part of a plant that grows underground. Roots take up water for the plant to use.

 **shoot** small green stem that grows from a seed

Index

Notes to Parents and Teachers

Before reading

Show the children an apple and ask them if they know how apples grow. Ask them what will be inside if you cut the apple open. Slice open the apple and look at the seeds together. What else do they know that grows from seeds?

After reading

• Talk to the children about the Jewish New Year, Rosh Hashanah. Explain how it is a tradition for Jewish people to eat apples dipped in honey during this festival so that they will have a sweet new year. Let the children dip a slice of apple each into some honey so they can try this.

• Tell the children the story of Johnny Appleseed and how he planted apple orchards in the United States. Talk about how important it is to plant new trees. Maybe you could plant an apple tree together in the school grounds.